CONNECT

BATTLE FOR A NEW NATION

CAUSES AND EFFECTS OF THE REVOLUTIONARY WAR

BY KASSANDRA RADOMSKI

Consultant:
Nathaniel Sheidley, PhD
Historian and Director of Public History
Bostonian Society
Boston, Massachusetts

CAPSTONE PRESS
a capstone imprint

Connect is published by Capstone Press,
1710 Roe Crest Drive, North Mankato, Minnesota 56003
www.capstonepub.com

Library of Congress Cataloging-in-Publication Data
Radomski, Kassandra.
Battle for a new nation : causes and effects of the Revolutionary War /
by Kassandra Radomski.
pages cm. — (Connect. The Revolutionary War)
Includes bibliographical references and index.
Summary: "Using the cause and effect text structure, explores how the Revolutionary
War began and its immediate and lasting effects"— Provided by publisher.
ISBN 978-1-4914-2006-5 (library binding) — ISBN 978-1-4914-2159-8 (pbk.) —
ISBN 978-1-4914-2165-9 (ebook pdf)
1. United States—History—Revolution, 1775–1783—Juvenile literature. I. Title.
E208.R13 2015
973.3—dc23   2014032762

Editorial Credits
Jennifer Besel, editor; Veronica Scott and Peggie Carley, designers;
Wanda Winch, media researcher; Charmaine Whitman, production specialist

Photo Credits
Bridgeman Images: ©Look and Learn/Private Collection, 26–27, ©Look and Learn/
Private Collection/Peter Jackson, 24 (left), ©Tarker/Private Collection, 41, Gilder
Lehrman Collection, New York, USA, 10, National Trust Photographic Library/
Attingham Park, Shropshire, UK/Sir Joshua Reynolds, 11, Peter Newark American
Pictures/Private Collection, 14, 21; Getty Images: MPI, 12–13, The New York
Historical Society, 43; The Granger Collection, NYC, 8–9,17,19, 29, 32–33, 40; Library
of Congress: Board of Inland Revenues Stamping Department Archives, Philatelic
Collection, The British Library, 15, Broadsides, leaflets, and pamphlets from American
and Europe/Printed Ephemera Collections, 24 (top right), Prints and Photographs
Division, 23, 31; National Archives and Records Administration: www.ourdocuments.
com, 38; National Park Service, Harpers Ferry Center, 16, Colonial National Historical
Park/Keith Rocco, artist, 4–5; Newscom: CMSP Education, 35, Design Pics/George
Munday, 6; North Wind Picture Archives, 37; Shutterstock: AridOcean, 44–45 (map,
Alaska), Atlaspix, 44 (Hawaii), Ekaterina Romanova (scroll design), Ensuper (multi
colored background), Extezy (calligraphic scroll), f–f–f–f (vintage calligraphic design),
nikoniano (grunge stripes), wacomka (floral design); Superstock: Superstock, cover

Printed in the United States of America in Stevens Point, Wisconsin.
092014   008479WZS15

TABLE OF CONTENTS

WHY WAR?

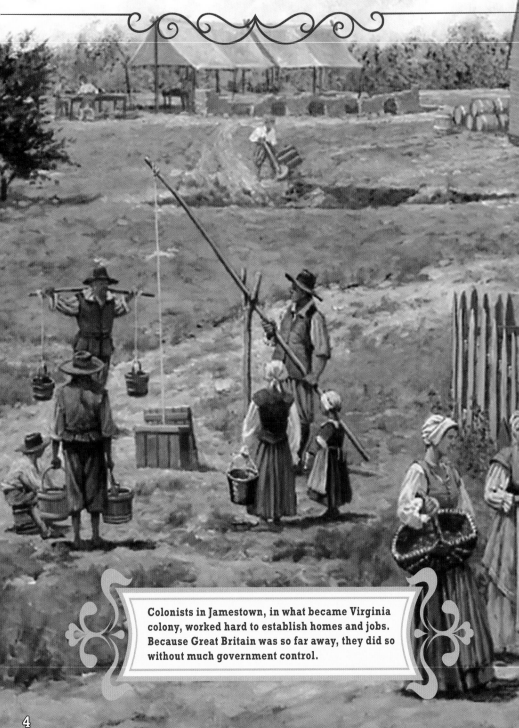

Colonists in Jamestown, in what became Virginia colony, worked hard to establish homes and jobs. Because Great Britain was so far away, they did so without much government control.

The Revolutionary War (1775–1783) began as a struggle between the world's most powerful country, Great Britain, and its 13 American colonies. Before the war Great Britain ruled over the colonies, and most colonists were proud to be British subjects. They also enjoyed the freedom of living in America—an ocean away from Great Britain's rule. But during the war, many colonists sacrificed their lives so the colonies could become independent from Britain. How did the once-proud British subjects get to the point of war?

The first colonists came to America in the 1600s. For the next 150 years, government leaders in London largely left the colonists alone. Each colony set up its own government and methods for collecting taxes. The money collected through taxes was used within the local colonies.

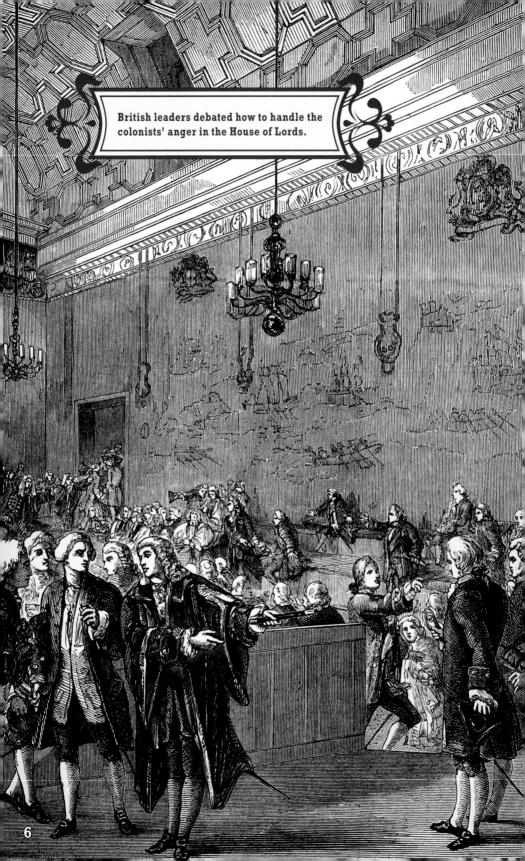

British leaders debated how to handle the colonists' anger in the House of Lords.

As Great Britain's empire grew, the task of ruling became harder. **Parliament** passed new laws that directly affected colonists. Great Britain showed it had ultimate power over the colonies.

Colonists felt like they were being treated unfairly. They had not elected any representatives to Parliament. So they didn't have anyone in the British government to defend their rights.

Their frustration turned into anger when British officials began inspecting ships carrying goods in and out of the colonies. Then Great Britain stationed its soldiers in the colonies. The tension between colonists and Great Britain grew and eventually led to war.

The American Revolutionary War wasn't caused by one event. Problems started with the French and Indian War (1754–1763) and continued with a long list of actions that caused violence and war to erupt.

Parliament—a group of people who make laws and run the government in some countries

CAUSES OF THE REVOLUTIONARY WAR

Cause 1 — THE FRENCH AND INDIAN WAR

The French and Indian War between France and Great Britain was a fight over land in America. The French claimed that the Ohio River Valley, the land between the Appalachian Mountains and the Mississippi River, belonged to them.

American Indians were already living on this land. Many Indians joined the fight, helping the French. They believed the French would help them keep the British from invading their lands. Great Britain and the colonists wanted this land for themselves.

After years of battle, Great Britain won the war and gained the Ohio River Valley. Colonists were eager to move onto this new land. But the British government objected. Despite the outcome of the war, some French settlers and American Indians refused to leave the area. Britain's Parliament feared another conflict would erupt if the colonists tried to move onto this land.

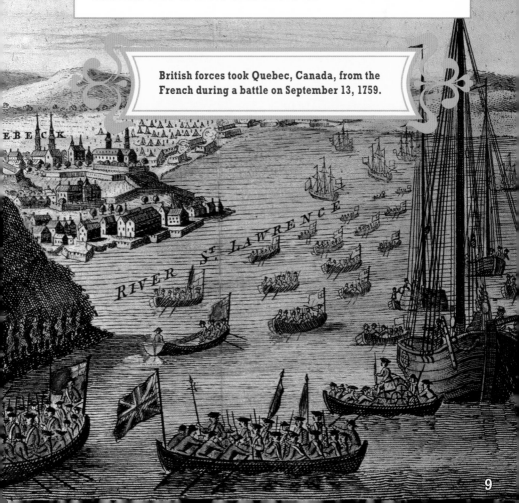

British forces took Quebec, Canada, from the French during a battle on September 13, 1759.

PROCLAMATION OF 1763

Soon after the war, the king issued the Proclamation of 1763. Part of this royal announcement prohibited colonists from settling west of the Appalachians. It also required any colonists who had already settled there to move back to the original colonies.

The Proclamation of 1763 also established colonial rule over former French and Spanish lands, including Canada and Florida.

The colonists were angry. They had gone to battle against France for this land. They felt the Ohio River Valley rightfully belonged to them.

Making matters worse, Parliament left 10,000 British soldiers in the colonies after the war. The troops were there to protect the colonists from future attacks from the French or American Indians. They were also there to stop colonists from moving west. These new restrictions planted the first seeds of ill feeling between colonists and Great Britain.

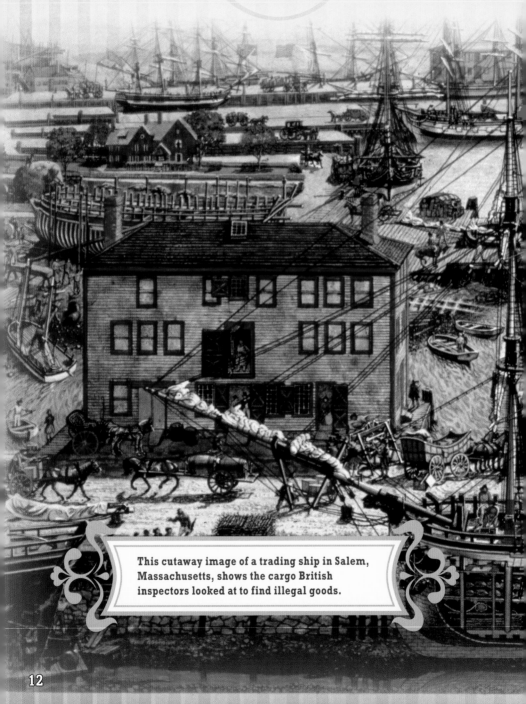

This cutaway image of a trading ship in Salem, Massachusetts, shows the cargo British inspectors looked at to find illegal goods.

The French and Indian War was expensive. When it ended Great Britain was in great debt. To raise money Parliament enforced a tax on goods such as sugar, coffee, and wine. Parliament also required inspectors to search ships going into and out of the colonies for illegal goods from other countries. Any colonists caught with smuggled goods were tried in British courts without a jury.

Parliament also passed the Currency Act in 1764. This law prevented colonists from using their own paper money. They were forced to use British money for all taxes and debts they paid to British merchants. The colonists were unhappy about these laws. They didn't understand why Britain was suddenly enforcing taxes and laws it hadn't before.

STAMP ACT

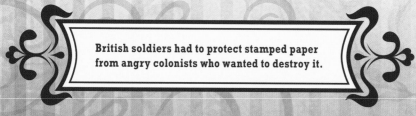

British soldiers had to protect stamped paper
from angry colonists who wanted to destroy it.

The Stamp Act of 1765 upset many colonists. This law required colonists to get a special stamp on paper items, such as newspapers, calendars, advertisements, playing cards, and legal documents. Colonists had to pay a fee for these stamps, and the stamps had to come from a stamp agent.

All the money raised through these stamps was used by Great Britain to help pay for the British troops in the colonies. British citizens thought it was fair that colonists pay for these troops. Soldiers were there to protect them. But colonists were outraged. They believed they were being taxed against their will.

the stamps put on newspapers in 1765

ANGRY REACTIONS

Some colonists reacted violently to the new laws and taxes. An angry mob in Boston broke a stamp agent's windows and destroyed his home. In New York angry colonists marched down the streets shouting, "Liberty!" and breaking street lamps. Similar reactions took place in other colonies. Stamp agents in every colony except Georgia quit their jobs. Colonists also boycotted British goods.

The colonists' anger toward Great Britain increased when Parliament passed the Quartering Act in June 1765. This law required colonial governments to provide British soldiers with food and a place to stay. Most colonists didn't want to feed these soldiers or provide them with housing. They didn't even want them in the colonies.

Colonists also destroyed Governor Thomas Hutchinson's home because they believed he supported the Stamp Act.

Sons of Liberty

Some colonists who opposed the Stamp Act formed a group called the Sons of Liberty. The group's members bullied British stamp agents into quitting and stopped colonial merchants from ordering British goods. They also published the names of anyone who did not follow along with the boycotts. Some of the group's most famous members included Samuel Adams, Paul Revere, and Benedict Arnold.

St—p!   St—p!   St—p!   No:

Tuesday-Morning, December 17, 1765.

THE True-born Sons of Li- berty, are desired to meet under LIBERTY-TREE, at XII o'Clock, THIS DAY, to hear the public Resignation, under Oath, of ANDREW OLIVER, Esq; Distributer of Stamps for the Province of the Massachusetts-Bay.

A Resignation? YES.

This poster from December 17, 1765, called a meeting of the Sons of Liberty in Boston. The Sons wanted local stamp agent Andrew Oliver to quit his job.

STAMP ACT CONGRESS

Many colonists believed if they worked together, they could force Britain's Parliament to reverse the Stamp Act. Colonists representing nine of the 13 colonies met in New York in October 1765 at the Stamp Act Congress. This group created a document that said only colonial **legislatures** could tax the colonists. Britain was violating the colonists' rights by taxing them when there was no one to represent them in Parliament. This idea was commonly referred to as "no taxation without representation." The Congress asked Great Britain to **repeal** the Stamp Act.

In 1766 Parliament did repeal the act. But the decision had little to do with the Stamp Act Congress. British merchants urged Parliament to repeal the Stamp Act because boycotts of British goods were hurting businesses. And there was another problem. Patriots had bullied stamp distributors so much that no one would take the job anymore.

When Parliament repealed the Stamp Act, it issued yet another law. The Declaratory Act made it clear that Parliament had ultimate authority in the colonies. The act said Parliament could pass other taxes or laws in the future.

legislature—a group of elected officials who have the power to make or change laws for a country or state
repeal—to officially cancel something, such as a law

the British Parliament in session

Townshend Acts

Year after year Parliament issued new taxes or laws that limited colonists' rights. With each new law, many colonists grew angrier. In 1767 Parliament passed the Townshend Acts. These new laws put taxes on glass, paper, paint, and tea. The law stated how much tax was placed on each item.

"For every hundredweight ...
of crown, plate, flint, and white glass,
four shillings and eight pence ...

"For every hundredweight ...
of painters colours, two shillings.

"For every pound weight ...
of tea, three pence.

For every ream of paper ...
twelve shillings."

The money raised through these taxes went to pay for the soldiers in the colonies. The colonists again responded by boycotting British goods. And anger began to boil over.

shilling—a coin that was used in Great Britain
pence—British pennies

THE PATRIOTIC AMERICAN FARMER.
J-N D-K-NS—N Esqr BARRISTER at LAW.
Who with Attic Eloquence and Roman Spirit hath Asserted,
The ... Colonies in America.

Dickinson's Essays

Many colonists expressed their dislike for Great Britain's laws and taxes by writing letters, essays, and books. John Dickinson, a well-known lawyer and politician, wrote a series of essays called "Letters from a Farmer in Pennsylvania." Dickinson's essays were published in colonial newspapers from 1767 to 1768. He believed British policies were wrong and took away colonists' rights. He urged colonists to take peaceful resistance. His writings had a major impact on colonial thinking. Today he is often called the "penman of the revolution."

Cause 3 — GROWING TENSIONS LEAD TO VIOLENCE

Patriots from all of the colonies expressed their anger with Great Britain. But Patriots in Boston were the loudest. They weren't afraid to express their outrage over the taxes, restrictions on trade, and the presence of British soldiers in the colonies. British soldiers were so disliked by Boston colonists that the soldiers were afraid to be out on the streets.

On the evening of March 5, 1770, a mob of angry colonists began insulting a British guard standing in front of a customs house in Boston. The crowd pelted him with snowballs and sticks. Eight other British soldiers soon came to the soldier's rescue. In the confusion the soldiers opened fire without their captain's command. Five colonists were killed. Others were injured. Patriots blamed the British soldiers for the tragedy, which became known as the "Boston Massacre."

Despite these events most colonists couldn't imagine being anything other than British subjects. Although they believed their rights were being violated, they weren't thinking about breaking away from Great Britain. What the colonists wanted most was for King George III and Parliament to listen to their concerns and recognize their rights.

Patriot—a person who sided with the colonies during the Revolutionary War

Fact

The first person shot in the Boston Massacre was
an African-American man named Crispus Attucks.

Artist F. T. Merril's drawing shows one
perspective of the events that came to be
known as the Boston Massacre.

a poster from 1773, detailing the new tax rules on East India Tea Company tea.

Many colonists began buying tea that had been brought in illegally from other countries in order to avoid buying East India Tea Company tea.

TEA ACT

On April 12, 1770, Parliament repealed most of the Townshend taxes except the tax on tea. The next three years was a period of calm in the colonies. The colonists returned to **importing** British goods. But bad feelings between the colonists and Great Britain brewed just under the surface.

Those bad feelings boiled up when Parliament enacted the Tea Act in May 1773. This new law was intended to help the British East India Tea Company get out of debt. No new taxes were added to those already collected. Instead, the East India Tea Company was allowed to sell directly to the colonies at a reduced rate. This made its tea cheaper than tea from other countries.

British leaders thought colonists would like the cheaper tea. But instead, many were furious, believing that Great Britain was trying to create a **monopoly** and control free trade. They feared Great Britain would try to control the trade of other goods too.

import—to bring goods into one country from another
monopoly—when there is only one supplier of a good or service

Some artists drew images of Patriots dressed as American Indians during the Boston Tea Party. Many of those images, such as this one, show the Patriots wearing headdresses that Great Plains Indians wore, which is not what happened. Historians now believe some Patriots wore one or two feathers, but no one was fully disguised as an Indian.

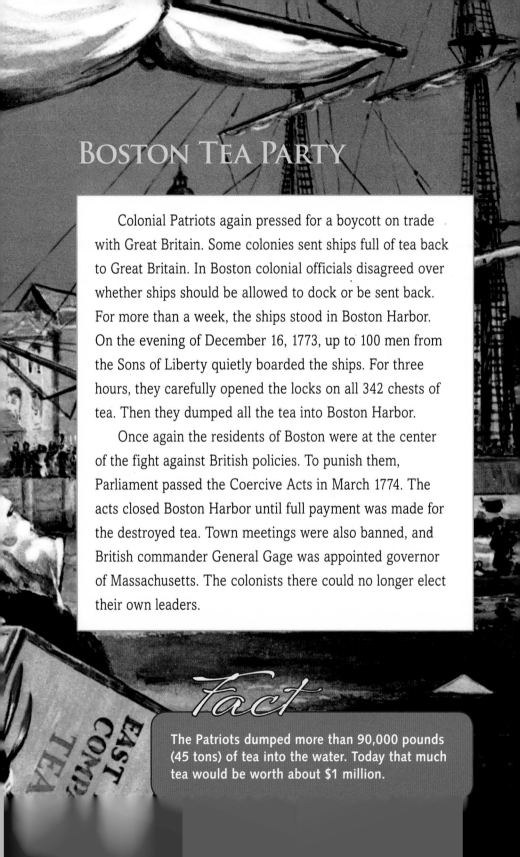

BOSTON TEA PARTY

Colonial Patriots again pressed for a boycott on trade with Great Britain. Some colonies sent ships full of tea back to Great Britain. In Boston colonial officials disagreed over whether ships should be allowed to dock or be sent back. For more than a week, the ships stood in Boston Harbor. On the evening of December 16, 1773, up to 100 men from the Sons of Liberty quietly boarded the ships. For three hours, they carefully opened the locks on all 342 chests of tea. Then they dumped all the tea into Boston Harbor.

Once again the residents of Boston were at the center of the fight against British policies. To punish them, Parliament passed the Coercive Acts in March 1774. The acts closed Boston Harbor until full payment was made for the destroyed tea. Town meetings were also banned, and British commander General Gage was appointed governor of Massachusetts. The colonists there could no longer elect their own leaders.

Fact

The Patriots dumped more than 90,000 pounds (45 tons) of tea into the water. Today that much tea would be worth about $1 million.

The Coercive Acts targeted Boston and left the other colonies alone. But the Boston Committee of Correspondence distributed letters reminding people that this could happen to them too. Soon colonists throughout America were fuming in what doctor David Ramsay called a "patriotic flame."

> "In the countries and towns of the several provinces, as well as in the cities, the people assembled and passed resolutions expressive of their rights and of their **detestation** of the late American acts of Parliament. These had an instantaneous effect on the minds of thousands. Not only the young ... but the aged ... joined in pronouncing [the Coercive Acts] to be unconstitutional and oppressive. They viewed them as deadly weapons aimed at the vitals of that liberty which they adored ..."

—from *The History of the American Revolution, 1789* by David Ramsay

detestation—to dislike someone or something very much

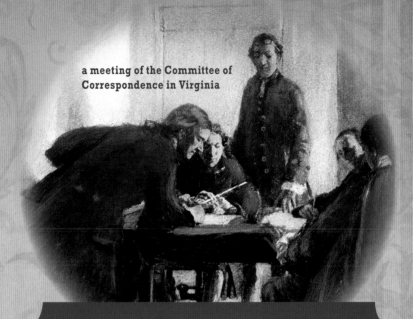

a meeting of the Committee of Correspondence in Virginia

Committee of Correspondence

Samuel Adams organized the first Committee of Correspondence in 1772. These committees were groups of colonists who met to try to resolve issues with Britain. They also joined together to talk about colonists' rights. Committees promoted their beliefs through letters, pamphlets, and newspaper editorials. In the years leading up to the war, committees met in every colony. The committees gave colonists a chance to voice their opinions and state their concerns about British policies. Coming together in this way led to a growing sense of colonial unity.

Fact

The colonists called the Coercive Acts the "Intolerable Acts."

FIRST CONTINENTAL CONGRESS

In 1774, 56 delegates from 12 colonies met in Philadelphia to form the First Continental Congress. Together they created a statement of the beliefs common among the colonies. They also listed their complaints against the British government. They criticized King George III for taxing the colonists without allowing them fair representation in Parliament. They stated their dislike for the British army in the colonies, which existed against their will. They issued a declaration of the rights all citizens should be allowed, which included life, liberty, property, assembly, and trial by jury. Finally, they asked King George III and Parliament to change their policies. The Congress declared an end to all trade with Britain until their demands were met.

King George III and Parliament completely ignored the complaints raised by the Continental Congress. The colonists were fed up with the way they were being treated. The voices of those who were in favor of independence grew louder.

Engraved by artist François Godefroy around 1782, this image shows a session of the First Continental Congress.

WAR

For years many colonists felt that war with Great Britain was the last resort. But over time many started to believe it might be the only solution. They began preparing for war. **Militia** companies formed. Colonists stockpiled ammunition. Parliament declared the colonies in a state of rebellion.

On April 18, 1775, Patriots learned the British planned to march that night to Lexington, Massachusetts. They were going to arrest Patriot leaders John Hancock and Samuel Adams. They were also planning to destroy a stockpile of ammunition in Concord.

militia—a group of volunteer citizens who serve as soldiers in emergencies

Paul Revere and William Dawes took off on horseback through the countryside, alerting townspeople to the British plan. Hancock and Adams were able to escape. And when the British arrived in Lexington, about 70 militiamen were waiting.

To this day no one knows who fired the first shot on that Lexington green. But someone did, and that shot started the Revolutionary War. When the battle was over, eight Minutemen were dead.

The British had won the battle. But as they marched back to Boston, more colonial militia swarmed them. The colonists attacked fiercely, killing and wounding more than 100 British soldiers.

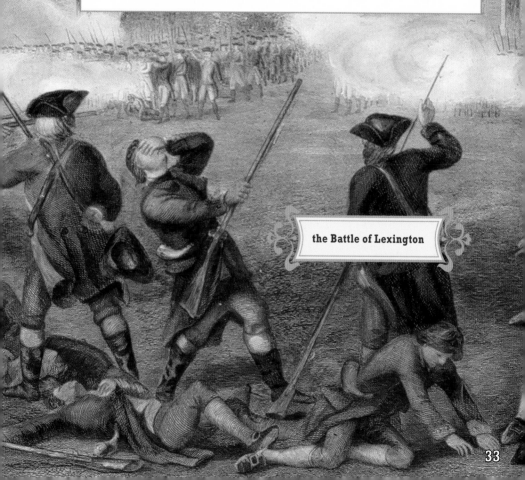

the Battle of Lexington

DECLARATION OF INDEPENDENCE

Patriots rushed to join militias. Loyalists joined with British troops. On May 10, 1775, the Second Continental Congress met in Philadelphia to discuss what to do now that war was upon them. Delegates voted to form the Continental army. They appointed George Washington the army's commander in chief.

Throughout the first half of 1776 battles continued to rage in the colonies. At the Continental Congress that June, a committee was formed to write an explanation of why the colonists had the right to declare independence. Committee members chose Thomas Jefferson to write the first draft. On July 2 Congress voted in favor of independence. On July 4, 1776, Congress adopted the Declaration of Independence, and several copies of it were printed. By signing the Declaration, the delegates officially declared independence and became British **traitors**.

Fact

Great Britain hired more than 30,000 German soldiers, called Hessians, to fight against the Patriots.

traitor—someone who aids the enemy of his or her country

signing the Declaration of Independence

END OF THE WAR

Colonists and British soldiers endured eight years of bloody battles. From north to south, the war touched every colony. But the colonists refused to give up, and the British refused to back down. Each side won and lost many battles.

Finally in October 1781 Washington secretly brought his troops to Yorktown, Virginia. The British had seized the city. But Washington's troops arrived in the dark of night and were able to trap them there. After several days of fighting, the British were forced to surrender.

The war was not over, but the British army was much weaker. Following this defeat Parliament began to discuss possible terms of a peace treaty. It grew clear to both sides that the Revolution was ending—and the Americans had won.

The British signaled their surrender with a drummer and a soldier carrying a white flag at the Siege of Yorktown on October 17, 1781.

EFFECTS OF THE WAR

the signed Declaration of Independence

Effect 1 AN INDEPENDENT SPIRIT

Delegates at the Second Continental Congress signed the Declaration of Independence. This document contains the guiding beliefs of American government. The second paragraph of the document declares,

> **"We hold these truths to be self-evident, that all men are created equal, that they are endowed by their Creator with certain unalienable Rights, that among these are Life, Liberty and the pursuit of Happiness."**

It also says government should protect the rights of the people, and that government's power comes from the approval of the people. This document stands as a symbol of the American spirit. People continue to use the document to defend America's actions throughout the world.

That independent spirit would also jump-start several movements within the United States in years to come. Abolitionists fighting to end slavery and women fighting for the right to vote used the Declaration to back their causes.

The U.S. government continues to draw from this belief in freedom as well. It continues to help other countries achieve their own independence. And the country's independent spirit has inspired many nations to model their ruling bodies after the United States' government.

The most immediate effect of the Revolutionary War was the creation of the United States of America. During the war delegates began to form a national government. They wrote the Articles of Confederation to guide the new nation. The Articles gave the most power to the states and not to a central government.

But shortly after the war, it became clear that the Articles could not keep the country together. They didn't provide the U.S. government with enough power to tax citizens or regulate trade. The colonial delegates tried to fix the Articles. When that didn't work, they created an entirely new document.

The U.S. Constitution created a president, Congress, and Supreme Court. It allowed the states to keep their own constitutions, but the U.S. Constitution became the highest law of the land. Adopted in 1788 this structure of national and state governments is still followed today.

Delegates debated the rules the new country would follow during the Constitutional Convention in 1787.

Effect 3

RELIGIOUS CHANGES

Religion played a major role in the Revolutionary War. Many people believed God was on the colonists' side, and that feeling helped boost the independent spirit.

Many colonists were members of the Church of England before the war. But as cries for independence turned to roars, members had a choice to make. The king was the head of the Church of England. Priests in the church had to swear loyalty to the king. And prayers said in the church asked God to give the king "victory over all his enemies."

Throughout the war the Church of England in America underwent many changes. Members began to omit the king's name in prayers. Many priests gave up their roles in the church because they could no longer be loyal to the king.

After the war the church reformed into a new American church. In 1789 members formed the Protestant Episcopal Church of the United States.

The Constitution was not a perfect document. It failed to address the issue of slavery in the United States. By failing to address this in the Constitution, slavery was common and legal for years after the Revolutionary War. Slavery would become a major issue that would bitterly divide the nation for decades.

Black Americans weren't the only people treated unfairly after the war. American Indians also suffered. The Treaty of Paris officially ended the Revolutionary War in 1783 and established the boundaries of the United States. But it did not protect American Indians or give them any rights to the land. Neither did the U.S. Constitution.

As Americans expanded west, they gradually forced American Indians off their land. Often Indians were forced onto government-approved land far from their homeland. Tension between the U.S. government and American Indian tribes would bubble for years, eventually leading to much violence and bloodshed.

Relations between Great Britain and America also remained tense after the Revolutionary War. Great Britain began to force U.S. sailors off their ships to work on British ships. These actions, along with the anger left from the war, would lead the two nations to battle again in the War of 1812 (1812–1815).

Most battles during the War of 1812 were naval battles fought at sea.

Free from British rule, Americans were able to expand their borders. They began to move west over the Appalachian Mountains. It didn't take Americans long to expand. By 1820 the size of the United States grew to 22 states with more than 9 million people. Over the course of 170 years, the United States grew to the 50 states it has today. It continues to be a country guided by the same beliefs Patriots spoke about—a country dedicated to equality and liberty for all.

In 170 years the United States grew from 13 colonies to 50 united states.

GLOSSARY

detestation (de-tes-TAY-shun)—to dislike someone or something very much

import (IM-port)—to bring goods into one country from another

legislature (LEJ-iss-lay-chur)—a group of elected officials who have the power to make or change laws for a country or state

militia (muh-LISH-uh)—a group of volunteer citizens who serve as soldiers in emergencies

monopoly (mun-AH-po-lee)—situation in which there is only one supplier of a good or service and therefore that supplier can control the price

Parliament (PAR-luh-muhnt)—a group of people who make laws and run the government in some countries

Patriot (PAY-tree-uht)—a person who sided with the colonies during the Revolutionary War

pence (PENCE)—British pennies

repeal (ri-PEEL)—to officially cancel something, such as a law

shilling (SHIL-ing)—a coin that was used in Great Britain

traitor (TRAY-tur)—someone who aids the enemy of his or her country

INTERNET SITES

FactHound offers a safe, fun way to find Internet sites related to this book. All of the sites on FactHound have been researched by our staff.

Here's all you do:

Visit *www.facthound.com*

Type in this code: 9781491420065

READ MORE

Forest, Christopher. *The Rebellious Colonists and the Causes of the American Revolution*. The Story of the American Revolution. North Mankato, Minn.: Capstone Press, 2013.

Gunderson, Jessica. *A Rebel Among Redcoats: A Revolutionary War Novel*. The Revolutionary War. North Mankato, Minn.: Stone Arch Books, 2015.

Perritano, John. *The Causes of the American Revolution*. Understanding the American Revolution. New York: Crabtree Publishing Company, 2013.

CRITICAL THINKING USING THE COMMON CORE

1. Explain how the French and Indian War changed the relationship between colonists and Great Britain. Use examples from this text or other sources to support your statements. (Integration of Knowledge and Ideas)

2. Discuss whether or not the Revolutionary War was a cause of the War of 1812. Use other sources to support your point of view. (Integration of Knowledge and Ideas)

3. Read the quotation from the Declaration of Independence on page 39. How did religion play a role in the creation of that document? Use this text and other sources to support your answer. (Integration of Knowledge and Ideas)

INDEX

Primary sources appear on the following pages:

Page 20, from The Townshend Revenue Act. June 29, 1767. Online by the Independence Hall Association. www.ushistory.org/declaration/related/townshend.htm

Page 28, from *The History of the American Revolution* by David Ramsay. (Philadelphia: R. Aitkin & Son, 1789.) Online by The John Adams Library at the Boston Public Library. archive.org/details/historyofamerica02rams

Page 39, from The Declaration of Independence: A Transcription. July 4, 1776. Online by The Charters of Freedom by the National Archives and Records Administration. www.archives.gov/exhibits/charters/declaration_transcript.html